Contents

What Is a Vitamin?

Imagine that your body is a machine. Your machine needs different fuels to run smoothly. These fuels are vitamins, minerals, **fats, protein,** and **carbohydrates.** Each fuel helps your machine in a different way.

OPPOSITE
Casimir Funk found that the outside layer of brown rice, called the hull, is rich in vitamin B_1.

Vitamins help make good use of food. Some vitamins turn food into **energy.** Others help you see in the dark or build bones.

A great discovery

People have always gotten vitamins from food. But it was not until 1911 that a Polish scientist named Casimir Funk proved that a substance in food affected people's health.

Funk was looking for a cure for a disease called beriberi. Japanese doctor Kanehno Takaki had already discovered that victims of beriberi ate lots of white rice. People who ate brown rice did not get beriberi. Funk studied the outer layer of brown rice, which is removed to make white rice, and found a chemical that cured beriberi.

The chemical he found in brown rice was not quite what he thought it was, but the name he gave it, "vitamine," stuck (the *e* was later dropped). We now know this chemical as vitamin B_1, or **thiamine.**

PRESENTED BY

Vitamins

by Rhoda Nottridge

Carolrhoda Books, Inc./Minneapolis

All words that appear in **bold** are explained in the glossary on page 30.

Illustrations by John Yates
Cartoons by Maureen Jackson

This book is available in two editions.
Library binding by Carolrhoda Books, Inc.
Soft cover by First Avenue Editions
241 First Avenue North
Minneapolis, Minnesota 55401

First published in the U.S. in 1993 by Carolrhoda Books, Inc.

Library of Congress Cataloging-in-Publication Data

Nottridge, Rhoda.
    Vitamins / by Rhoda Nottridge.
      p.   cm.
    Includes bibliographical references and index.
    Summary: Focuses on vitamins, explaining why we need them in our diet, where we can get them,
and the different kinds.
    ISBN 0-87614-795-3 (lib. bdg.)
    ISBN 0-87614-610-8 (pbk.)
    1. Vitamins in human nutrition—Juvenile literature.
[1. Vitamins.] I. Title.
QP771.N64   1993
615'.328—dc20   92-21415
                                                                                  CIP
                                                                                   AC

Printed in Belgium by Casterman S.A.
Bound in the United States of America

1   2   3   4   5   6   98   97   96   95   94   93

The Vitamin Cure

Following Casimir Funk's lead, many doctors and scientists began to search for vitamins that would cure other diseases.

Vitamin C

Scurvy was a disease that caused weakness, loose teeth, and sores. Sailors on long voyages often died from it. People knew that the disease was connected to the limited **diet** sailors had, so sailors made sure to eat fresh meats, vegetables, and fruits when on shore. The fresh foods helped, but no one was sure why.

In the 1740s, a Scottish doctor named James Lind gave sick sailors citrus fruits along with their normal diet. The sailors began to recover

BELOW
When these lemons ripen, they will be an excellent source of vitamin C.

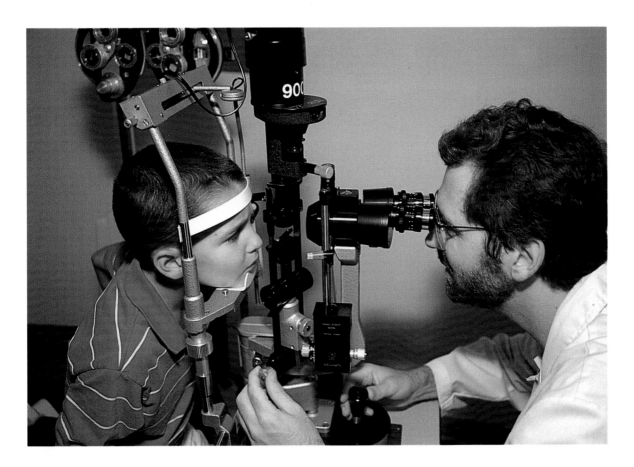

almost immediately.

From then on, although no one knew exactly why limes prevented the disease, British ships carried limes or lime juice on voyages. Until 1932, when a Hungarian scientist discovered the chemical **ascorbic acid,** or vitamin C, some people believed fresh foods of any kind were the cure for scurvy.

British sailors are still called "limeys" after Dr. Lind's cure.

Vitamin A

For thousands of years, people have suffered from an illness called night blindness. These people have poor eyesight and cannot see well in the dark.

In 1907 Dr. Elmer V. McCollum found that rats who ate only grains, such as corn and wheat, first became night blind and then completely blind. But a diet containing green leaves, butter, and cod liver oil restored the rats' sight.

ABOVE
Getting regular eye exams and eating foods rich in vitamin A will help your eyes stay healthy.

7

Dr. McCollum then found the chemical, which he named the "A-factor," or vitamin A, in the butter and oils, but not in the leaves. Finally, seven years later, he discovered **carotene** in green and yellow vegetables. Our bodies use carotene to make vitamin A, or **retinol.**

The B vitamins

In the early 1900s, a disease called pellagra spread rapidly among poor people in the southern United States. Victims developed nausea and rough, red skin and eventually died. In 1913 Dr. Joseph Goldberger found that cornmeal was often the only food pellagra victims could afford to buy.

When Goldberger visited an orphanage, he found that the children between ages 6 and 12 all had pellagra. Very young children and children old enough to have jobs and buy food for themselves were healthy—and both healthy groups drank milk. The difference was vitamin B_2, also called **riboflavin,** which Goldberger found in 1928. By 1933, he found that his "B_2" was really two vitamins: B_2 and B_3, or **niacin.**

There are now more than eight B vitamins, known together as vitamin B complex.

Vitamin D

For years parents made their children take cod liver oil to prevent a disease called rickets. This disease softens bones in children, causing them to have bowlegs and curved spines. Children given daily doses seemed less likely to get rickets.

In 1919 Dr. McCollum, who had discovered vitamin A in cod liver oil, set out to see if vitamin A was also the cure for rickets. But he found out that the oil worked even with the vitamin A taken out. There had to be another vitamin in the oil.

In 1922 McCollum discovered vitamin D. Later scientists found that our bodies can make vitamin D by themselves using sunlight.

Scientists have learned a lot about vitamins since they were discovered. They know where each vitamin can be found and how our bodies use those vitamins.

Vitamin A: the Sight Vitamin

ABOVE
Watching TV in a dark room uses up a lot of vitamin A.

Have you ever heard that eating carrots will help you see in the dark? It's true! Carrots are a major source of carotene, which our bodies use to make vitamin A. Vitamin A is sometimes called the sight vitamin because it helps keep our eyes healthy.

People who don't get enough vitamin A may have difficulty seeing clearly in the dark or when lighting changes. Their eyes may also feel dry and itchy.

However, vitamin A not only helps our eyes. Vitamin A is important for normal growth and healthy bones, teeth, and skin. Vitamin A even helps protect our bodies from the air pollution and germs we breathe.

Some other foods high in carotene are spinach, sweet

Science Corner

To learn more about where different vitamins are found, look on the packages of the foods you eat. Cereal boxes are a good place to start.

Some vitamins are known by a full name rather than a letter or number. Learn to recognize these names on package labels so you can tell exactly what the foods you eat contain.

Then make a chart like the one below, filling in the names of the vitamins and where you found each of them.

	Ascorbic acid	Folic acid	Niacin	Riboflavin	Thiamine
	(Vit. C)	(B group)	(B group)	(B group)	(B group)
Where it is found	tomato soup		cornflakes	cottage cheese	ham

potatoes, squash, apricots, and melons. High levels of vitamin A in its natural form (not as carotene) are found in liver. Other natural sources include milk and butter.

Vitamin A stays in our bodies for a long time because we use it very slowly. This means that we don't need as much of vitamin A as we do of some other vitamins.

11

The B Vitamins

Vitamin B complex is made up of at least eight vitamins, all of which work together closely. The most important of these vitamins are thiamine (B_1), riboflavin (B_2), niacin (B_3), B_6, B_{12}, and folic acid. They work together to maintain the health of our **nervous system,** skin, and **digestion.** The only foods that contain all the B vitamins are liver, **wheat germ,** and **brewer's yeast.**

Sunflower seeds, brown rice, and other grains that have not been **processed** are good sources of vitamin B_1.

Vitamin B_2 is found in high doses in kidneys and dairy products, especially whole milk.

Lean meats, fish, and peanut butter contain large amounts of niacin.

Vitamin B_6 is found in carrots, potatoes, and fish.

Vitamin B_{12} can be found in eggs, milk, liver, and other animal products. Because few plants contain B_{12}, **vegetarians** need to make sure they get enough of

ABOVE *A piece of bread loses one-third of its vitamin B_1 when it is toasted.*

it. Two Japanese seaweeds called wakame and kombu are good plant sources of B_{12}. They are sold at health food stores. Brown rice, peanuts, and sunflower seeds also contain B_{12}.

B_{12}, along with folic acid, prevents anemia, a blood disorder. The body stores B_{12} for some time, so we do not need to eat it every day.

Eating green leafy vegetables gives us the folic acid we need. Pregnant women and young children especially need plenty of this vitamin.

While all of these foods contain B vitamins, they may be lost if food is overcooked or left in the sun.

Science Corner

Bean sprouts are an excellent source of vitamins. They taste good on sandwiches and salads. Why not add bean sprouts to your diet by growing them yourself? You'll need a half cup of mung beans (sold at health food stores) and a glass jar with a lid.

1. Put the beans in a cup or bowl and cover them with water. Leave them to soak overnight. 2. Drain the beans and put them in the jar. Cover the jar and place it in a warm, dark place. 3. Rinse the beans twice a day with warm water and drain them well. 4. In a few days, the shoots should be about two inches long and ready to eat.

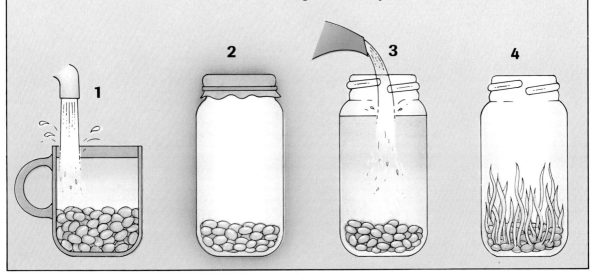

Vitamin C: the Cold Cure?

Most animals make vitamin C in their bodies. But humans, as well as apes and guinea pigs, are different. We need to get vitamin C from the foods we eat.

Vitamin C has many uses. It helps to heal cuts, bruises, and burns. It is important for the growth and health of our teeth, gums, blood, and bones. One of its most important functions is to help the body fight illnesses.

Some scientists believe that we can avoid getting colds and can cure them faster by taking large doses of vitamin C.

We are not yet sure if this is true, but our bodies do need more vitamin C when we are ill. This is because the body uses up vitamin C fighting illnesses.

Studies are also being done to investigate possible links between vitamin C and asthma, arthritis, gum disease, and certain kinds of cancer.

Fresh-squeezed orange juice contains more vitamin C than any other food. Other citrus fruits and their juices, as well as berries, green peppers, and tomatoes, also contain large amounts of vitamin C.

However, simply eating one of these foods does not guarantee that you will get all the vitamin C it once contained. Time is one thing that destroys the vitamin. Foods lose vitamin

BELOW
Eating an orange is a quick and easy way of getting vitamin C.

C as they get older. For example, a newly dug potato will contain three times as much vitamin C as a potato that has been stored for the winter.

Vitamin C also dissolves in water, so when fruits and vegetables are cooked in water, they lose their vitamin C.

No one knows exactly how much vitamin C our bodies need. However, we do know that the body does not store it, so we need to make sure that we get some every day.

ABOVE
Fresh-squeezed orange juice is a healthy and delicious alternative to processed soft drinks.

Drink Your Vitamin C

Many fruit drinks sold in stores have been processed, so many of the vitamins the fruits contain have been destroyed. Here's how to make lemonade that is delicious and full of vitamin C.

You will need:

4 fresh lemons
3 cups cold water
½ cup sugar
2 tablespoons hot water

1. Cut the lemons in half and squeeze them over a pitcher until you have squeezed out all the juice (about 1 cup). 2. Remove seeds from lemon juice. 3. Mix sugar together with hot water and add to lemon juice. 4. Add cold water and stir until well mixed. 5. Chill lemonade for at least one hour. Now it is ready to drink!

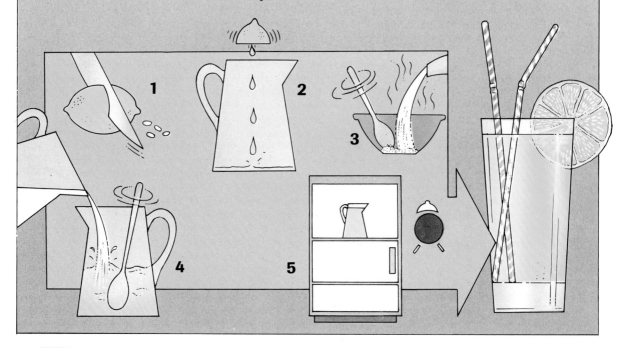

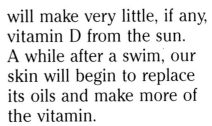

Vitamin D: the Sunshine Vitamin

Vitamin D is not only found in food, nor is it only made by our bodies—it's both!

Vitamin D is often called the sunshine vitamin because we can get it from sunlight. In the sunlight, the oils in our skin work with the sun's rays to make vitamin D. But if we swim or have a bath before going out in the sun, we wash away the oils in our skin, and our bodies will make very little, if any, vitamin D from the sun. A while after a swim, our skin will begin to replace its oils and make more of the vitamin.

Elderly and disabled people who rarely go outside may not get enough of the sunshine vitamin. People who live in countries where there is not much sunlight, such as England, are less likely than those who live in sunny countries to get enough vitamin D.

Vitamin D can be found in food, too, but largely in foods most people don't eat much of: oily fish, such as herring, mackerel, and salmon, and cod liver oil. Milk is enriched with vitamin D, but you would have to drink eight glasses to equal the vitamin D in three ounces of herring.

Most people get enough vitamin D. Without it, children may get rickets. In adults, this disease is called osteomalacia. Both diseases result in brittle, painful bones.

BELOW
Sunlight is good for our bodies because it gives us vitamin D. But we still need to wear sunscreen to protect our skin from the sun's strong rays.

Vitamin E

People have called vitamin E a "miracle" cure for all sorts of things, but no one really knows what it does or how it works. Research has suggested that vitamin E encourages the growth of new cells in the body.

Some people have found that their scars and wrinkles faded a little when they rubbed them with vitamin E cream. This made them believe that enough vitamin E would keep them looking young forever. Vitamin E will not make skin look young again, but it does seem to make burns heal

LEFT *This boy uses vitamin E cream to help cure a skin problem called eczema.*

faster when the vitamin is put on right away.

Other studies suggest that vitamin E may help the body fight heart disease and cancer, and the effects of chemo-therapy and air pollution.

Vitamin E is found in wheat germ, nuts, and vegetable oils.

Looking Good with Vitamins

Vitamins are as important to our appearance as they are to our health. Look carefully at this chart. Now think about your own body. Do you have strong nails? Are your teeth healthy? Is your hair shiny? If you answered no to any of these questions, you may not be getting enough of some vitamins.

Vitamin A Helps keep hair, scalp, eyes, and skin in good condition. A lack of vitamin A may cause dry skin and dandruff.

Vitamin B Maintains the correct level of oil in the skin. Too little vitamin B may cause poor hair growth or dandruff.

Vitamin C Keeps skin firm and hair, eyes, and teeth healthy. It also helps us recover from illness. Bruising and broken veins are a sign of a shortage of vitamin C.

Vitamin D Makes nails, teeth, and bones strong. A lack of vitamin D may cause soft, ridged nails, tooth decay, or rickets.

Vitamin E Helps heal burns and soften wrinkles. A lack of vitamin E may cause brown "age spots" on older people's hands.

How Many More Vitamins?

There are two more vitamins that are so common that we do not need to worry about getting enough of them.

Vitamin K is the most common of these vitamins. Foods that provide vitamin K include green vegetables, dried beans and peas, meats, dairy products, and eggs.

This vitamin helps our blood to clot, or thicken, to stop a cut from bleeding.

The substance called vitamin P is not really a vitamin at all. It is actually a group of substances that is found in foods that contain vitamin C. This group, called bioflavonoids, seems to help vitamin C work properly.

The vitamins B_{15}, B_{17}, and U are called vitamins, but no one knows if they are necessary for good health and worthy of their name.

Studies have found that B_{15} may help control epileptic seizures. Russian scientists have believed for years that B_{15} improves athletic performance. But B_{15} has not been proven safe to use. More tests are needed to find out what it really does.

Scientists also need to do more tests on B_{17}. Some studies show it helps fight cancer, but it also contains a dangerous chemical called cyanide. B_{17} is illegal in the United States.

Scientists believe cabbage contains a substance they call vitamin U. Drinking cabbage juice may reduce the pain of stomach ulcers. So far no one has learned how to remove vitamin U from cabbage for testing.

Minerals

Minerals are different than vitamins because they come only from soil. We get minerals by eating plants or by eating herbivorous, or plant-eating, animals. Minerals work with vitamins.

BELOW
Calcium helps to make our teeth strong, but we need to clean them regularly to keep them healthy.

Mineral Needs

Write down what you have eaten so far today. How many of these five minerals did your meals contain?

Can you think of other foods you could have eaten instead to make sure you had enough of all five of these important minerals?

Minerals	Needed for	Found in
Calcium	Healthy bones, teeth, muscles, and blood; well-running nervous system	Tofu, cheese, yogurt, milk, ice cream, green leafy vegetables
Iron	Healthy blood	Liver, seafood, green vegetables, dried fruits
Phosphorus	Strong bones and teeth, removing energy from food	Milk, cheese, yogurt, eggs, meat, fish
Sodium	Nervous system, muscles, and the balance, or amount, of water in the body	Salt, cheese, processed foods, bacon, cured fish
Potassium	Nervous system, muscles, water balance in the body	Fruits, vegetables, nuts, wheat germ

Our bodies need small amounts of about 17 minerals. Minerals that affect our bones and teeth are calcium, phosphorus, and magnesium. Iron, sodium, and potassium are needed for healthy blood.

Some minerals are only needed in very tiny amounts, but they are still important. These minerals, called **trace elements,** include copper, zinc, magnesium, and fluorine. The other minerals found in our bodies do not seem necessary for good health.

Vitamin Supplements

There are two ways to make sure that you get enough vitamins and minerals. The best way is to make sure to eat a balanced diet that contains all the different vitamins. If you are unable to get all your vitamins this way, you may need to take vitamin **supplements.** Supplements got their name because they supplement, or add to, your diet. They should be used in addition to, not instead of, a healthy diet. Ask an adult before taking any vitamin supplement.

BELOW
Vitamin supplements come in liquid, pill, and powdered forms.

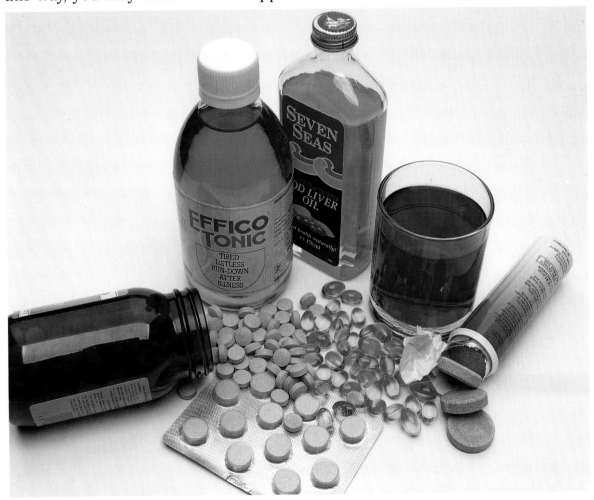

Since scientists first discovered vitamins, they have found ways of singling out, or isolating, vitamins. One way is by removing vitamins from foods. Another way is to use chemicals to copy the vitamins' structures. These isolated vitamins are made into pills, liquids, and powders.

Scientists and doctors disagree about how safe vitamin supplements are. Some feel that extra amounts of certain vitamins, such as vitamin C, will make a person more healthy. Others think too much of any vitamin may be harmful. But the one thing they all agree on is that too much of vitamins A and D can be dangerous.

One way to know how much of each vitamin you should get each day is to follow the **recommended dietary allowance (RDA)** established by the U.S. Food and Drug Administration for each vitamin and mineral.

This information can be confusing, because RDAs are determined using unusual measurements. More helpful are the percentages of RDAs listed on most packaged foods.

Another simple guideline is to eat at least four servings each of dairy products, breads and cereals, and fruits and vegetables every day. You should have at least two servings of meat, eggs, and legumes, or beans.

BELOW
Garlic is sometimes made into pills that are good for the blood.

Groups at Risk

When you are young, it is very important to make sure you get the vitamins and minerals you need to grow.

Other groups of people also need to take particular care. For example, teenage girls often do not get enough vitamins or minerals. They need plenty of iron and vitamins A and B_2. Calcium and vitamin D are also important—for teenage girls and all young people.

Athletes need to make sure they get enough vitamins to keep their strength up. B vitamins are particularly important. Vitamin B_1 is lost through sweating. Hard exercise burns a lot of vitamin B_2.

Adding more of these vitamins to your diet will not make you a better athlete, but eating more foods rich in vitamin B will make you more energetic.

BELOW
A healthy diet containing all the important vitamins will help you keep fit.

The Basic Four

For the next week, keep a record of everything you eat. Then use this chart to see how healthy your diet is. Try to eat a variety of foods within each food group as well as the number of servings suggested. If you got enough servings from each of the four basic food groups each day, you probably got the vitamins you need.

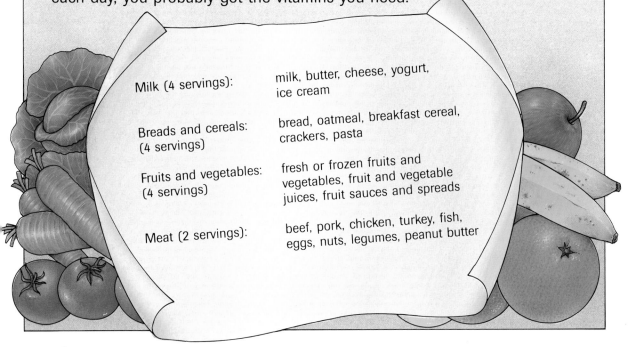

Milk (4 servings):   milk, butter, cheese, yogurt, ice cream

Breads and cereals: (4 servings)   bread, oatmeal, breakfast cereal, crackers, pasta

Fruits and vegetables: (4 servings)   fresh or frozen fruits and vegetables, fruit and vegetable juices, fruit sauces and spreads

Meat (2 servings):   beef, pork, chicken, turkey, fish, eggs, nuts, legumes, peanut butter

But never increase your intake of just one B vitamin. Always be sure to increase the others too, since the B vitamins work together.

Elderly people need extra vitamins because they eat less than younger people and their bodies are slower at using the vitamins in food.

Dieters who are cutting down on what they eat need to take care that they are not cutting out important vitamins. Strict diets that only allow you to eat a few different foods almost never provide enough vitamins.

Smokers actually lose vitamins when they smoke. No matter how balanced one's diet is, just one cigarette will destroy a full day's vitamin C.

Vitamin Destroyers

As you've learned, we can get all the vitamins we need from a balanced diet. However, much of the food we eat today is processed. When food is processed, it is cooked, dried, or changed in some other way to make it easier for us to prepare. But processing often destroys or removes vitamins and minerals.

Even when we avoid processed foods, we should be careful that the processing we do when we cook at home does not destroy the vitamins.

Prepare food only when you are ready to cook and eat it. If you need to store cooked foods, put them in sealed containers in the cupboard or refrigerator, where the foods will be protected from light and air. If foods must be prepared ahead of time, sprinkle salads and fruit with a little lemon juice to seal in vitamin C.

Avoid soaking or cooking fruits and vegetables in water. Instead, rinse fruits and vegetables well and steam them in a tightly covered pan on a rack over—not in—boiling water. This preserves vitamins B and C. Do not peel foods such as potatoes and apples that have edible skins. Also be careful not to overcook foods.

BELOW
Meals at fast-food restaurants often contain highly processed foods.

By following these guidelines, you and your family will be well on your way to a healthier lifestyle.

Meal Planning

It is easy to read through a list of foods containing all the important vitamins. It is much harder to make sure your diet contains them all.

With a friend, plan a menu for either breakfast, lunch, or dinner. Try to make sure the meal contains as many as possible of the vitamins and minerals necessary for good health.

The menu below is what a healthy lunch might look like.

MENU

A glass of milk.
(vitamins A and D, calcium, potassium, phosphorus)

Tuna salad on whole wheat bread (vitamins A, B, C, and E, iron)

Apple or Orange (vitamin C)

Glossary

Brewer's yeast A powder high in B vitamins that was once used in brewing beer

Carbohydrates The nutrient, found in foods such as sugars and starches, that supplies the most energy

Diet The foods a person eats

Digestion The process of breaking down the food we eat into nutrients such as vitamins and minerals

Energy Power made by your body from the food you eat and the chemicals in your body

Fat The high-calorie nutrient that is the most efficient source of energy

Nervous system The network in the body that controls feeling and movement

Processed Stripped of its healthfulness by the way it was prepared

Protein A nutrient found in meat and vegetables that is the building block for every part of the body

Recommended dietary allowance (RDA) The amount of each vitamin and mineral considered necessary for good health

Supplement A source of vitamins or minerals that is taken in addition to food

Vegetarian A person whose diet contains no meat

Wheat germ A grainy food made from wheat kernels

Books to Read

Citrus Fruits by Susan Wake (Carolrhoda Books, 1990)

Eggs by Dorothy Turner (Carolrhoda Books, 1989)

Fish by Elizabeth Clark (Carolrhoda Books, 1990)

Food and Digestion by Jan Burgess (Schoolhouse Press, 1988)

How to Eat Your ABC's by Hettie Jones (Four Winds Press, 1976)

Vegetables by Susan Wake (Carolrhoda Books, 1990)

The Vitamin Puzzle by Malcolm E. and Ann E. Weiss (Julian Messner, 1976)

Metric Chart

To find measurements that are almost equal

WHEN YOU KNOW:	MULTIPLY BY:	TO FIND:
AREA		
acres	0.41	hectares
WEIGHT		
ounces (oz.)	28.0	grams (g)
pounds (lb.)	0.45	kilograms (kg)
LENGTH		
inches (in.)	2.5	centimeters (cm)
feet (ft.)	30.0	centimeters
VOLUME		
teaspoons (tsp.)	5.0	milliliters (ml)
tablespoons (Tbsp.)	15.0	milliliters
fluid ounces (oz.)	30.0	milliliters
cups (c.)	0.24	liters (l)
quarts (qt.)	0.95	liters
TEMPERATURE		
Fahrenheit (°F)	0.56 (after subtracting 32)	Celsius (°C)

Index